THE AMAZING ADVENTURES OF

Ellie's Best Beach Vacation Ever

Co-Author and Assistant Photographer - Elle Fair
Co-Author and Photographer - Marci Fair
Assistant Editor - Chloe Fair
Cover and Layout Designer - Cornelia G. Murariu

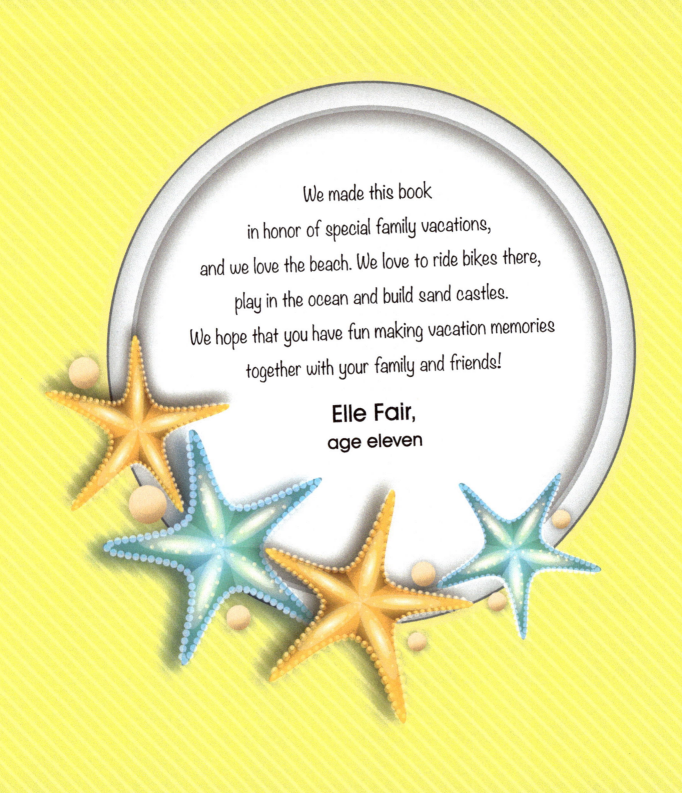

We made this book
in honor of special family vacations,
and we love the beach. We love to ride bikes there,
play in the ocean and build sand castles.
We hope that you have fun making vacation memories
together with your family and friends!

Elle Fair,
age eleven

Ellie and Pudgy could not wait to leave for their beach vacation. They tried on their new sunglasses, picked out some beach toys and finished packing their suitcases. As soon as they were in the van, Ellie asked "How much longer until we get there?"

When they arrived, Ellie and Pudgy wanted to go play at the beach right away.

They looked through all the colorful
beach toys and chose their favorites.
They were ready to walk to the beach.

To get there, they first walked down a brick path under a lot of trees.

Then they got to the boardwalk and saw the gate to the beach—they were so excited to almost be there!

As they walked through the gate,
they stopped at the top of the stairs.

They could not believe how white the sand was,
and how beautiful the blue and green water was.

They liked to dig in the white sand and build things.

Ellie loved to swim and Pudgy loved to snorkel in the ocean.

It was fun to see fish friends swimming in the water with them!

All that playing, digging and swimming made them hungry.

They chose the perfect food for lunch—friendly froggie pasta.

That afternoon, it was time to visit their favorite book store. It was very comfortable and full of so many wonderful books!

Ellie and Pudgy even made some more new friends there. They love to read books, so it was fun to search for some great new ones.

The next day, Ellie and Pudgy decided to go ride bikes, one of their favorite things to do. They biked in between homes.

They biked on the board walks.

They biked down a narrow alley. They biked between plants and flowers that smelled so good!

They biked on "secret" paths no one else knew about. "Shhhhh!" Ellie said. "Don't tell anyone about the secret paths!"

Riding bikes was fun to do with a friend, good exercise, and a great way to explore the little beach town.

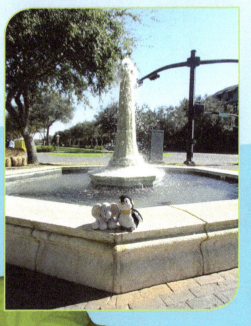

After biking, Ellie and Pudgy walked around and found a lot of bubbly fountains. There were tall ones and short ones...

...there were even ones with goldfish in them.

Then they discovered the play ground. It had so many fun places to climb. They both fit perfectly on the tire swing. They loved to swing high!

The slide was so big Pudgy's glasses fell off on the way down. The playground was so fun!

 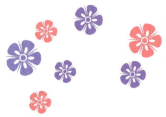

The next morning they found a small, special Butterfly Garden just around the corner. It was full of all kinds of plants and flowers that butterflies liked.

Ellie liked the purple flowers. Pudgy liked the bright pink ones.

They did not see any butterflies there, though. Maybe it should be called the "un-butterfly garden!"

Ellie and Pudgy went back to the beach to build a sand castle. They started out with one small one.

Then they kept building and building...

...and building...

They built until their very little sand castle became a very BIG sand castle! We all have to start small, to grow something big.

Soon Ellie and Pudgy were hungry for an afternoon snack.

There were so many special, yummy treats at the ice cream shop, it was hard to choose the perfect thing.

Ellie chose her favorite snack—ice cream. Pudgy put her favorite chocolate candies on top to share!

To cool off that afternoon, they went for a swim at the pool.

They even took a short nap on the lounge chair.

Everyone loves to relax on vacation.

Their amazing trip to the beach was coming to an end.

They went to the board walk to watch the last sun set.

As the sun went down over the ocean water, the sky turned so many beautiful colors, like the colors in the rainbow.

Ellie and Pudgy would never forget
their vacation at the beach…

…and they were already counting
the days until they could come back.

"Share Your Favorite Stuffed

1

Set up your favorite stuffed animals making vacation memories together.

2

Take a photo or ask someone to help you take one.

We will recognize your creativity and will love

Animal Friends Too!"
Here's how in four easy steps:

3

Upload and share your photo on our page,
Facebook.com/ellieandpudgy

4

Tell us their names and type hashtag #elliesfriends

MEETING YOUR FAVORITE STUFFED ANIMAL FRIENDS TOO!

Dear Parents,
Vacations big or small, long or short, at home or away, all make special family memories. The most important factor is the time together. We hope that you find fun, simple ways to enjoy your vacations. We would like to say a special thank you to our favorite beach bookstore, The Hidden Lantern, for their hospitality and excellent taste in books! (www.TheHiddenLantern.com)

Congratulations to Rosemary Beach for 20 years of great memories! 1995 - 2015
www.rosemarybeach.com

The Amazing Adventures of Ellie The Elephant:
Ellie's Best Beach Vacation Ever

Copyright ©2015 Marci Fair, Pacochel Press LLC
All rights reserved.
First Edition

Printed in the United States of America

Permission to reproduce or transmit in any form or by any means—electronic or mechanical, including photocopying and recording—or by any information storage and retrieval system, must be obtained by contacting the author by email at info@guiltfreemom.com.

Ordering Information
For additional copies contact your favorite bookstore, online store, or email info@guiltfreemom.com.
Special offers for large orders are available.

ISBN-10:0996363521
ISBN-13:978-0-9963635-2-5

More of Ellie's Amazing Adventures Coming Soon!

www.EllieAdventures.com

CPSIA information can be obtained
at www.ICGtesting.com
Printed in the USA
JSHW021047200819
1141JS00001B/4